If All the World and Love Were Young

IF ALL
THE
WORLD
AND
LOVE
WERE
YOUNG

STEPHEN
SEXTON

WAKE FOREST UNIVERSITY PRESS

First North American edition
First published in Great Britain by Penguin Books in 2019

For permission, write to:
Wake Forest University Press
Post Office Box 7333
Winston-Salem, NC 27109
wfupress.wfu.edu
wfupress@wfu.edu

ISBN 978-1-943667-08-6 (paperback)
LCCN 2023945270

Designed and typeset by Peter Barnfather

Publication of this book was made possible by
generous support from the Boyle Family Fund.

In memory of my mother for my father for my brother

Photography is seen as an acute manifestation
of the individualized "I," the homeless private
self astray in an overwhelming world.
– SUSAN SONTAG

Yet I cannot escape the picture
Of my small self in that bank of flowers:
My head among the blazing phlox
Seemed a pale and gigantic fungus.
– JOHN ASHBERY

It's a-me, Mario!
– MARIO

NOTE

In the summer of 1998, when I was nine, my mother took a photograph of me playing *Super Mario World* (1990) in the small spare room in our house. My back is to the camera. The television was positioned so it faced out from the corner of the room where the wall met the patio door. To my left, I could see the garden, along which a little river ran and, over the fields, a dense forest. To my right, there was the huge block of the television, which was already fifteen or sixteen years old. My eyes drifted between these two positions. Because of the flash of the camera and the glare of the television screen, it's impossible to tell which of the following levels I'm playing.

The Super Nintendo is a 16-bit console. Put simply, 16-bit refers to how much memory the system can process at one time.

PART ONE

Yoshi's Island

Yoshi's House

These are the days of no letters the magenta mailbox jitters
out of the visible spectrum babies chirp in our holly tree
mountains yield to the foreground and sadly again they're beautiful:
my friends scattered in the lowlands the fire seizes in the grate
the smoke signals across the eaves say all I really mean to say
I have gone to rescue my friends I'll think of you and you and you.

Yoshi's Island 1

Here spotted mountains and cirrus here sloping plateaux
      drawn down on
carnivorous plants and no sun gold by the cherish underground
fly agaric throbs everywhere with fire plants and dinosaurs.
In these days new as tomorrow there is joy to be recorded:
the tender steps in other lands all the flowers of the garden.
My mother winds her camera the room is spelled with sudden light:
a rush of photons at my back a fair wind from the spectral world.
I remember myself being remembered a little lotus
a cross-legged meditant for whom the questions floating in the air
are for a future self to voice decades from now who will return
again and again to this room and these moments of watershed.
It will be an adventure I think it will be an adventure
the future is cannon blasting yes I must have dreamt this her voice
narrows into dreams of such things ships sink at the edge of the world.

Yellow Switch Palace

On Kappa Mountain past the great lake circumscribed with goldenrod
the abandoned palace is full of treasure glowing underground
in granaries and arsenals an economy of losses
and gains the beloved is gone but there is always the story.
Should a Kappa step out of myth made of scales and razory claws
a shell of keratinous scutes the hard beak of an octopus
and a vulnerability to kicks on the top of the head
should he step wet out of the lake I will offer to him kindness.
I will offer soba noodles in soy I will offer my name
written on cucumber floated on the lake whatever the cost.

Yoshi's Island 2

Pixels and bits pixels and bits their perpendicularity:
one of the worlds I live in is as shallow as a pane of glass.
The threshold of the window sets a frame around the holly tree
wild funguses slimy with dew and toxicity the rubies
of holly berries sing on the branches the robins hide among
and the veins of ivy vines wind around the slumping trunk and boughs
sloe berries in the blackthorn and the carcinogenic bracken.
Groundsels loiter along the low dashed wall the daisies loll about.
One summer's day I'm summoned home to hear of cells
     which split and glitch
so haphazardly someone is called to intervene with poisons
drawn from strange and peregrine trees flourishing
     in distant kingdoms.
We take the air in the garden bitter with berries and mushrooms
too toxic to eat where the grass bows in an unexpected breeze.

Yoshi's Island 3

Today I climbed the Windy Mount the highest peak in this region.
My singular wish was to see what its elevation offered.
With one companion my brother who is no better or worse than
anyone else I saw blankets of mushroom fields reducible
to patchworks what the birds' eye view must see of farms in Genoa.
I went so far up the broken path I supposed I should almost
see the curve of the planet or the whim on which the waves begin
but for the first time in some time I thought of our father at home
the Sirocco in from the south turtle doves in the huge wheat fields.

Yoshi's Island 4

Salt water everywhere low tides undulate a flotsam of mines
the archipelago aswim with joyful blue-white puffer fish
and in a neighboring province saguaro prowl a feline prowl.
An ovale lagoon on the peninsula buoyed us as children
aboard a heavy pedalo the likeness of a giant swan
almost unmaneuverable about the tropical island
silly with plastic palms and shale from whose hollow we called to land
to our mother on the seafront between the artificial pool
and the sunstruck coastal waters who beckons us back to harbor.
Since it's August she begins the idle effacement of dying
the many prickles of needles of many exotic compounds
hormones and corticosteroids the stiffening of the larynx
mouth the dry of the walk alone into the desert finding there
those cactuses their open arms and their long curious shadows.

#1 Iggy's Castle

My dreams reply the garden has become an ocean of lava
a precinct of spewing tephra the rock like black honey folding
over again impossibly and yet on a shaky island
someone stands surrounded by fire who says to go without me.
So there is a sound in the house when I wake mice under the moon
my mother who cannot sleep halves a bright grapefruit
      whose feet whose toes
whose hands whose fingers whose ankles whose head
      she says are on fire.

Donut Plains

Donut Plains 1

The land of flight feathers no birds backstop Chuck chucks
      his knuckleballs
the shrubs are off the Scoville scale. The little house on the border
keeps a mantelpiece abrim with porcelain knick-knacks Delftware dust
sixteen ceramic cows rowboats on the lake in gray photographs.
The lie of the land is the shape of the north of Ireland likewise
missing a lump from its body: and the lake fills with eels zigzagged
from the Sargasso like needles of glass light slowed through sodium.
The little house on the east shore of the lake has something in it.
The chimney trickles smoke the hearth interprets cords of sycamore.
This is not our house but its walls are flowered with our images:
us as babies pink and sleeping and as children formally posed
in green and red fleeces zipped up to the chin in any weather
the questionable fashions of the early nineteen-nineties
sepia-warmed wedding pictures before I found myself alive
the glowing eyes of relatives whose faces are written in light.

Donut Plains 2

Henry goes west on a ship to meet the Blue Mountains of Sydney.
Henry goes south and burns in the sun through Canberra to Melbourne.
The Princess of Tasmania docks and Henry sails aboard her.
Henry goes down in the mines of Tasmania for zinc and lead.
It is 1964 and collapse collapse Henry is dead.
20 or so years and she gives me her brother's name to mine with.
Down I go with bats and pyrite slow progress and landslides inching
canary-yellow minerals words do not contain their echoes.
Jacques says a name contains something like an abyss I wonder Jacques.
Somewhere underground a treasure chamber is dumb with emeralds:
where are you you might ask aloud where are you it might answer back.

Green Switch Palace

The stone cottage long abandoned by disenchanted farmers' sons
crumbles is unsalvageable its acreage dreams of limestone
yet it has in it echoes of *far other worlds and other seas*
annihilating all that's made to a green thought in a green shade.
Mosses explode within its walls: hunter shamrock harlequin mint
emerald persian paris lime chartreuse viridian midnight.

Donut Ghost House

What is there to be afraid of? Whatever moves in the rafters
a sparrow's nest in the chimney stuck with hay and pigeon feathers
a knock knock knock on the slate roof is hello yourself long ago
and hello an afterimage after all one image pressed to
and escaping through another. As the world of the living peers
out into the world of the dead as the isle is full of noises
as the draft catches the blue door as its keyhole's made of nothing
as the fireplace crackles and offers the light of the forest
the sparrow leaves its nest of eggs or maybe the sparrow doesn't.

Top Secret Area

I have been trying to tell you the secret of infinite lives:
she plants roses in the garden she pliant flows in the journal
she plants roses in the garden sea plants wrasses in the ocean
she plants roses in the garden she paths road signs from the station
she plants roses in the garden sea plans ruses in the argot
she plants roses in the garden seaplanes rising from the water
she plants roses in the garden sea froze rolling in the harbor
she plants roses in the garden see pain trilling in the garden
she plants roses in the garden shc planes ruins in the jargon
she plants roses in the garden see plinths raising in devotion

Donut Secret 1

I only know the night birds by their lullabies which echo through
the darkened fields and countryside like shepherds singing anything
they can to keep themselves awake: the names of all the villages
and towns they'll visit homewardly the names their children
        might have had
the names of all the fish they know who unlike me are fast asleep:
wrasses sleep tilapia sleep the hogfish sleeps the dogfish sleeps
the catfish sleeps the salmon sleeps the tuna sleeps the sunfish sleeps.
And sleep do the millions of eels from the Sargasso like needles
the kelp ripples in the current and I have been holding my breath.
Anglerfish doze in the trenches luminescent esca glowing.
Night itself sleeps sweet on my chest and she quarters
        a bright grapefruit.

Donut Secret House

The little house on the east shore of the lake has something in it.
It is nighttime when I arrive a mist settles against the roof
picture windows in wooden frames return my image in their glass
the dashed gray brick worries off here and there a giant fruitless bush
almost a story high leans on the western wall or does the wall
whose foundations bear high water when the floods come annually
gales when the season supposes it lean against the giant bush?

Donut Secret 2

It is winter in the Ulster Hospital and winter outdoors
and winter in our hemisphere the tilt of the planet says so.
Since she has lost her sense of taste we have dinner in McDonald's.
If I'm going to die she says might as well go to McDonald's.
The kitchen bleeps and chirps and blips the cryptolect of ICU's
whose automatic song desires no singer's articulation.
Her hair is thin under the light and surgery will be discussed
tonight while fleets of gritters salt all the main arterial routes.
The country roads we travel home by purple and glisten with frost
underneath the constellations and the Sagittarian moon.

Donut Plains 3

The bridge is split and trussed oak trunks laid across the gorge the water dapples against the edges of imagine the sheer drop the bridge swaying in the southwestern wind the white-clawed sea skulking below. One thing must become another chop chop the tree becomes a bridge forest becomes a labyrinth whose prospect one climbs higher for and from the falling dream you jolt somehow having landed having been nowhere but long in front of the beautiful television.

Donut Plains 4

Those blue afternoons of winter the air crisp and cool as thinking.
Kappa swarmed in every color under a waxing crescent moon
which seemed to augur well for me once I was falling to my death
once I survived the fall landing in a trench scooped and jigsawed out
of the earth hello earth nice to see you amazed to be alive
where chestnuts roll around and others parachute from trees.
During the dark century's wars I read children filled their pockets
with chestnuts to render into acetone to render into
cordite into shells sitting primed in the rifles of their cousins.
What will be the consequences of the trees waving in the wind
chestnuts in the hospital grounds the low dazzling winter sun?

#2 Morton's Castle

The wind blew as it blows over the ramparts and the battlements
along the merlons and crenels the fieldwork of Morton's Castle.
A wind jigs on the lake surface a dilemma sharpens its horns.
The castle is riddled with traps where boulders grin and bounce below
a mace that swings in rotary its fullest circle pendulum
and glassless gothic window frames in ancient hallways long as dreams.
In the castle is the surgeon lean and elegant as a fork.
This is how it's done precisely he says sharpening his finger
to a point so fine it's finer than any sparkle in his eye.

Vanilla Dome

Vanilla Dome 1

Now we must beware of the cave after a few days of fasting
the anesthesiologist apothecaries carefully
and the personable surgeon goes under the skin precisely.
I go down into the dark mines where my name clings like a horseshoe
and deeper until the stream of my blood runs as black as the coal.
In Kimberley diamonds grow in the walls for thousands of years.
The mines dug out by hand have left countless thousands
      dead having not
chosen the underground if they could help it. And so diamonds
is what I think of diamonds without a thimbleful of light
beautiful time goes by slowly and the surgeon covers his tracks.

Vanilla Dome 2

The Big Hole was excavated 240m
deep but has since filled up with rain water and general run-off.
It's this I think of: paddling on its azure eye lazily
in some leaky rowboat Sundays from now when the whole thing's over
and I'll say wasn't it strange how we used to live like that? And she
will say do you think it's strange to miss yourself? as the sun goes down.

Red Switch Palace

The Big Hole was excavated when there was something there to want.
Spelunkers marvel at its size but overlook the Sharashka
built into the basin. It's said there are prisoners kept even
now alchemists smashing rubies into dust into medicine
as though dabbing it on the tongue might remedy hematomas
as though wearing the grains of it might render one invincible.

Vanilla Secret 1

The sun tugs fistfuls of ivy and vine stems to the cave's ceiling.
I take the Orpheus route from one world up into another
via footholds and fissures and bone dry mouths in the sheer rock's face
into the brightly lit-waiting room and something like wakefulness.
From the window one sees new wards under construction skeletal
scaffolds and platforms the tang of diesel fumes miserable clouds
chainsaws buzzing in the distance and she wakes to car after car
bringing women and fatherly men who will turn into fathers.

Vanilla Ghost House

The nurses' watch fobs hang upside down so we sleep all day like bats
and weep all night in the private room while the steady drip of morphine
renders us half there and half not. The ghostly nurses roam around
in an old house stoking the fire dusting the furniture creaking
along the halls and calling out to those whose absence keeps them there
in white nightdresses their oil lamps held up to their glowing faces.
Moonlight seeps through the window as quick and silver as mercury
to tell us one hand is too hot and the other clean as a knife.

Vanilla Dome 3

A suit of salamander skin and gloves of stitched and softened tongues
and tail-lined slippers tough and fair to wear across the streams of fire.
His raft become automated poor Charon dosses on the banks
a penny here a penny there I would give him for his troubles.
And Dante has under it all a kingdom of ice their breaths clear
in the air down the ragged fur they climb up into the morning.

Vanilla Dome 4

A few stars are still vibrating and through the fields behind our house
the fox hunt tramps in uniform khaki drab fatigues desert boots.
They march as far as Solitude Bridge where the quarry blackly looms
and enter the woods with blunt-nosed and agitated scouting dogs
with their small caliber rifles high-powered dazzling floodlights.
I know the narrow path they take the little lake with fewer swans
year after year and fewer trout past the marshes and bulrushes.
It's the narrow path between sleep and wakefulness any minute
a gunshot the roar of a swan a stillness deeper than before.

Vanilla Secret 2

I think of the Alps edelweiss the ibex wildly scaling crags
and cliff edges but most of all I think of Ötzi the Iceman
lying in wait these few thousand years with hop-hornbeam in his gut
flax and poppy and sloe berries reaching out of the frozen earth
extending a frail hand as if to say I'm here it was lonely
I have longed for how it feels to be seen by someone else's eye.

Vanilla Secret 3

Arion crossing the Strait of Messina set upon by thieves
maniacal for blood and gold offered them a final music
to choose the terms of one's own death is handsomer than golden rings
he might have sung towards the prow and recognizing destiny
between two waves stepped overboard not to drown but be delivered
onto dry land by a dolphin enchanted by this final song
since he was the finest player of the cithara of his day.

Vanilla Fortress

I'm swimming with the coelacanths rotting in the flooded fortress.
The unbeautiful things propel themselves in flat trajectories.
So many years we have missed you little fish little Lazarus
fossil-king of the underbite not that you knew you were missing.
They will not see me swimming here: the darkest fathoms of the keep
where spikes are falling from the roof and bone-machines
      roam dismally
among spine-topped anemones marauding on the castle floor.
To suffer suffer everywhere and not a moment stop to think
let the world go on without me the next life will find me happy
and adrift pedaling the swans some bright day the sun names the boats
one by one in the marina this will have been so long ago
by then and I will have missed you for so long will I have missed you.

#3 Lemmy's Castle

In blue scrubs the Merlins apply various elixirs potions
panaceas to her body some hemostatic medicines
and a soupçon of opiate. The hospital's huge boiler plant
rumbles hums like a volcano the wards sweltering greenhouses
where all the patients start to look the same they are gradually
replaced cell by corrupted cell. At bedsides of parents children
hold it together their children play games on their little handhelds
young faces lit up in the light oblivious to the passing
moments since there is the question now of Lemmy is in his castle
hiding among the heating vents confusing us with his body
doubles we would know anywhere that smile or pool of lava or
protruding from the row of pipes those legs like Breughel's Icarus.

Twin Bridges

Cheese Bridge Area

Why does it have to be like that? Why does what have to be like that?
Cracker Barrel. It's a weird shape. Well I don't mind. Does it matter?
No other cheeses are that shape. Some other cheeses are that shape.
It's not that really. It's just square. Well it doesn't taste square. It's cheese.
Maybe it's the square/cracker thing. Well not every cracker is square.
The crackers in the cupboard are. There are other kinds of crackers.
Maybe it's the Barrel part then. Well what's the problem with barrels?
I dream of someone throwing them. Do you know someone
      who does that?
It seems like a long time ago. It has nothing to do with cheese?
No the cheese just reminded me. Cheese can mean almost anything.

Cookie Mountain

Now that the cancer's been excised the clouds are almost meaningless
a sparrow's not a metaphor for shipping out on rocky seas
there is no creaking in the house. So I crush biscuits in a bag
add sugar and golden syrup raisins heave the mess in a tray.
Since she can't stand for very long I make tiffins for the bake sale.
No one is going to like this I say but I have done my best.
She prints her name unsteadily on a white adhesive label
for the biscuit tin that had been her mother's before it was hers
her mother's before it was hers: snow-topped mountains circling birds.

Soda Lake

The little rill of our river runs a mile or so to the lake
that we some Sundays would walk to. Sometimes fly-fishers
     on the banks
catching nothing drinking cider but flinging their damsel lures out
again and again and further. Sometimes no one but us feeding
heels of loaves to the ducks coursing in a chevron on the water
which is mostly murk and algae. Some nights it is not uncommon
to hear a salvo of gunshots bounce all along the river's length
the way a cat brings home the gift of a bird bloodied still alive.

Butter Bridge 1

Yes something to do with balance. One foot in front of the other
over the hump of the stone bridge the water slowly dismantles.
A transformer hums near it now where a scots pine shrugs overhead.
It's something to do with balance or it's nothing to do with it.
The way pylons repeat themselves across the fields of Herefords
the young among them gamboling then the whole herd stopped
       and staring
all those pairs of eyes bewildered the way pylons repeat themselves
a crooked line of ancestry a chain of association:
the flowers of apple blossom and apples cored in the kitchen
the pips like painted fingernails the boy kept black until the end
slowly unwoven by cancer on the inside at least he kept
the body he could see stylish at sixteen that is important.

Butter Bridge 2

The traffic on the Albert Bridge crawls stubbornly from the city.
Crews are coxed along the river by a voice through a megaphone.
This is I suppose what faith is a voice that steers into the dark.
A murmuration of starlings is a smudge on the setting sun
or the huge and happy thumbprint of Shigeru Miyamoto.

#4 Ludwig's Castle

This is the dream: it is of stone corridors of carnelian
and jasper infinite for all I know and spiked maces swinging
in the rusty reddish half-light the still air of an ossuary.
There is music too concerti and sonatas overtures suites
the acoustical buzz of skulls their jawbones almost sing along
and I almost hear the voices of the dead crow gloomy mordents
a jumble of hemiolas then the wail of an elephant
in the despair of C minor and there's him at the piano
banging away at the keyboard and spooking out the symphony
which more resembles the Virgin and Child carved out of ivory.

Forest of Illusion

Forest of Illusion 1

Whatever language the trees speak in the temple of the forest:
the knot of dark eyes signaling in the goat willow's eastern skin
or the spiny caterpillar making letters on the branches
it is familiar to me as sunset must be to nightfall.
Not to be read but understood says the trickle of the river
and without saying anything on the tree lands the butterfly
some call the Camberwell Beauty and others call the Mourning Cloak.

Forest of Illusion 2

Catkins drop into the river their spines gone limp they float along
its course and wind up in the lake where the rainbow trout
   spawns in spring.
I caught one once with an old rod of fiberglass and a fat worm
almost split in half on a hook and wriggling for all it was worth.
Under the dark surface flashes of color the hook speeding off
like a silver key on the line until I stopped it with a flick
of the wrist and hoisted the fish from one world and into the next.

Blue Switch Palace

Colors sounds perfumes correspond hedgehogs wander
      the woods at night
as loud as newborn children's hair or singing like the fallow fields.
Some bird is cawing amphibrachs the color of the gibbous moon
a mouse is coinage in the yard like motor oil or six bright stones.
Like six bright stones are sweet as milk the owl can see for sixteen reds
an insect moving through the grass and swoop down like
      a broken chord
and sleep then like a bag of bulbs while hedgehogs slowly start to rain.

Forest Ghost House

Nature is a temple of trees oboes pass the time in boxwood
I go along the narrow path so faint it's hardly even there
until the wilderness gives way to a paddock part barbed wire
part palisade where the only sound is of the passing river.
Trotting through the fenced-off clearing shoeless and a barrel of ribs
emaciated rheumy of eye fearful of its own body
the turmoil of its aching flanks and rickety legs a white horse.

Forest of Illusion 4

She plants roses in the garden now that the wound is almost healed.
With a little trowel I dig and bury the bulbs she scatters.
It's like another life she thinks the days go by in gratefulness
with amber incense gooseberries growing on gooseberry bushes.
She will not be the same of course but nor will anybody else.
Now that the wound is almost healed the nights go by so silently
that if you tried you'd almost hear the roses sleeping in their bulbs.

Forest Secret Area

High above the forest one sees the curve of the peninsula.
A farmer continues to plow whose workhorse walks dully along.
A shepherd looks out for the wolves that skulk through
      crags and crevices.
An angler seeks out plump brook trout. A Spanish galleon lingers
hugely in the bay the white sails burly with wind the conifer
mast holding snedded of branches and needles on the forest floor
the rigging like a piece of gauze in sweet and favorable winds.

Forest of Illusion 3

It's almost the end of summer and Saturday the radio
in the kitchen is a havoc of Omagh way beyond the lough
and of Slevins the chemists' shop of children running in the road
of a group of a Spanish tourists of the Assumption of Mary
insofar as it can be seen. I pause in the darkened forest.
With a dram of soap and water my brother blows bubbles all day
each of iridescent shimmer each a shallow breath in transit

Forest Fortress

We go together to the church on the hill over the village
the wild country green behind it. In other places it's not noon
but here it is the coffin rests with a wealthiness of flowers.
My mother was a child with her. How quickly fifty years can go.
I am the light of the world says the sermon the stained glass window
says St. Peter with rays of light. The first color television
she ever saw was in her house my mother says and we all stand.

#5 Roy's Castle

The house's windows are undressed and with her old-fashioned Singer
she's putting stitches in some bolts of blue fabric the small piston
fires all through the evening and its industry of needles
runs a track through the radio softly playing Roy Orbison.
The whole world could be this one room she'll in a future return to
the curtains she's making all drawn against the light against July
the sewing machine ticks so fast these small years go by in minutes.

Chocolate Island

Chocolate Island 1

The rhinoceroses dodder like a basso ostinato
in the valleys between mountains in their scooped-out eroded cirques.
If there is magic in their horns they seem indifferent to it
trudging along instead upon the khaki-colored mountain path.
I want to call them dinosaurs but that's not even kind of close:
those hundreds of millions of years that supercontinental break.
In Queensland there was that fossil showing a dinosaur stampede:
hundreds of sharp little talons but no sign of what had spooked them.
Thousands and thousands and thousands and thousands
      of lifetimes ago
these glyphs are all they've left behind. One clear night not so long ago
we all stood out in the garden wondering up at the comet
whose memory is very long who we hope still remembers us.

Choco-Ghost House

And now there's this pain in my side like a bird in the holly tree
like there was something on fire. Look how the rainclouds have lifted
like a bird in the holly tree there one moment and gone the next.
Look how the rainclouds have lifted. I'm thinking of a storm in Spain
there one moment and gone the next. I can't forget the lightning though.
I'm thinking of a storm in Spain and us on the wet balcony.
I can't forget the lightning though forks flashing again and again
and us on the wet balcony playing card games with the damp deck
forks flashing again and again. The huge trees came down around us
playing card games with the damp deck. Power lines toppled
     like ships' masts.
The tourists all ran in the streets like there was something on fire.
Power lines toppled like ships' masts and now there's this pain
     in my side.

Chocolate Island 2

As Dürer sees it under the hides of carburized iron thick
as armor plating fixed in place with rivets pinned along the seams
a polished gorget at the throat the rhino is mostly passive.
What he got wrong hardly matters since he'd never seen one himself
having just a poem a sketch imagination to go on
making magic of the mundane. And so the sun sets in the west
which is to be expected there over the marshes and deltas
I should like to describe to you having never seen them myself.

Chocolate Island 3

Sallie Gardner at a Gallop shows the horse with all four hooves off
the racetrack at Palo Alto California only in
frames 2 and 3 of 24. But I have known this all along
she might have told us if she could on this day half the way through June.
This was the year the Wright brothers saw a little helicopter
made of bamboo cork and paper with coiled rubber for a rotor
and started drawing up blueprints to leave the earth altogether.

Chocolate Secret

The precipice overlooks the valley mystic with shadow where
I glimpse again the other world a creature pacing back and forth
in a keep illuminated by the flickering of neon.
That the world unmercifully will not end is the hardest thing
that the world will go on without you and on beyond a black day
of terrific rain umbrellas snapping billowing overcoats
a day which somehow has in it the day she drove home with this box
seat-belted in the backseat this world the apparatus of love.

Chocolate Fortress

On a beautiful day in June we take the pain to hospital.
In through the automatic doors along the dull linoleum
past chaplaincies and children's art the infirm and the elderly.
Somewhere in the sky hangs Saturn planet of melancholia
malefic of black bile and drear. With his stethoscope slung around
his broad shoulders like an athlete with a towel Hippocrates
says for now the pain must stay here in the small room without flowers.
A bell does not begin to toll a goat does not begin to bleat.
In the forbidden pharmacy he goes about the magic task
of grinding down a rhino's horn to infuse with ground down rubies.

Chocolate Island 4

Fossicking in the mines again for citrine amethyst rose quartz
over the pools of sleech and sludge at this the nadir of the earth.
I walk the gravelly hillocks like one who walks a pilgrimage
down the long slide to crappiness it is supposed to be painful.
The spiked rocks of the cave floor sit like rotten teeth in rotten jaws
I walk on the rocky tongue of the planet in its open mouth
under the sad wild fearful eyes of Saturn devouring his son.

Chocolate Island 5

The sprites move in cells no taller or wider than their own bodies.
Many-faced mountains are jagged and complex as lumps of bismuth
the ashen land looks fire-struck and dry as the Atacama
with its mirages shimmering so convincingly I could pike
into puddles of water fronds of eelgrass swaying and come up
for air years ago in the pool of the La Mon Hotel into
its thirst and sting of chlorine and its something about to happen.

#6 Wendy's Castle

The afternoon is bright and clear as a bell tolling on the hour.
Music seeps from a radio playing at the nurses' station:
some Wendy sings her final songs in a voice low as a whisper
as bright as a shower of sparks sheared off in a welder's workshop.
Patients shuffle by with their bones emerging from their thinning skins
from the necklines of their kirtles their blue cotton hospital gowns.
So we wait in the private room turn the egg timer of ourselves.
Hippocrates in his white coat brings with him a shake of the head
brings with him the word for sorry which is the word for we have done
everything within our powers we have shaken out our potions
we have cast our shining magic and where we cannot do some good
at least we must refrain from harm. And the traffic lights are changing
and the traffic will dribble on along the busy carriageway
towards the beach or barbecues because it's the summer solstice.
And then the talk of opiates of comfort and what's possible
of a cloak threaded with morphine another castle to die in.
I'm sorry she wanted to say my body won't cooperate
my body's become overcome though she did not say anything
but stared as if to recall how my face looked when she first saw me.

Valley of Bowser

Sunken Ghost Ship

Not a warship but a merchant brigantine adrift disheveled
but seaworthy with no crewman or passenger footing its decks
having set off for Genoa from New York many years ago.
The story goes the ship was found abandoned in beautiful trim
with every sail set not a rope out of place fire in the grate
400 miles from the Azores. The passengers weren't seen again.
Deep blue sea I ask no questions of you deep blue sea tell no lies.
Still here swells a sense of falling down through the bottom of the world.
One takes a last breath of this world and closes one's eyes and descends.

Valley of Bowser 1

Like a labyrinth of neural pathways one encounters dead ends
and blind alleys and cul-de-sacs all of which are really the same
save to say there are various ways of finding oneself lost there:
lost like rain on the Atlantic lost in the garden I planted
my name I wrote on old cardboard I remember now the shepherds'
red sky and all through to morning the secateurs snapping thickly
and when a woman came to cut our hair she seldom remembered
our names mistaking my brother for me for a pair of scissors.

Valley of Bowser 2

On through the valley of shadow shifting strata mazes of dirt
walls closing like mine collapses or morphine's tightness in the chest
its heaviness and its terror. A fountain drips in the courtyard
birds do motets and madrigals although the birds are seldom seen.
Some things we choose to disregard: the cruelty of newspapers
the casual chat of holidays the world and how it now appears.
Henry comes up how young and fine and dead now nearly fifty years.
How the telegram sent received said only YOUR SON HENRY DEAD.
How expensive to correspond all that way from Tasmania.
This is how the visitors talk without saying what they're thinking.
After not so long she's dozed off. The ancient voice of her brother
who wanders through the corridors takes on the clean sound of scissors
or the sound of water leaking from the mouth of a broken tap.

Valley Fortress

These are the days of no letters her signature starved with jitters
in the few half hours she's awake to make arrangements: no flowers
no more than is natural for a swift discreet funeral
and burial with her parents tea and sandwiches afterwards.
She sleeps the undertaker leaves the fountain leaks in the courtyard.
My head is heavier than stone. I read yesterday's newspapers
eat crisps from the vending machine I want to die is what she says
not either asleep or awake let me please die is what she says.
It's me I'm here is what I say but I am not since she is not.
Then she says I want to go home once more for one once more one night
and I say you can't go home now she says I know not now after.

Valley Ghost House

Bright brother it is you I seek in the cobwebs in the alcoves
as though images of us still roam there or are in the future.
Anyway should you some evening hear that creak or keen of timber
on the landing think of the house we grew up in the begonias
patterned across the stairs the fuzz of the carpet against your cheek
think that this creaking now is just us long ago when we were young:
the toy trains zooming through the rooms the secret door
        in the hedgerows
where hosts of robins passing make exactly the sound of the wind.

Valley of Bowser 3

It's so short she says it's so short it doesn't feel like I've been here
at all and now I have to go. The bluish light is from a lamp.
The portable television we brought from home is standing by.
I won't get to see what happens to you or your brother she says
as if our lives were determined already along one sure path.
No grandchildren and no first steps and never again a first word.
My first word she says was apple or something something like apple.

Valley of Bowser 4

So it's one who wears a cuirass who spends the evening throwing stones
from the vantage-points afforded by his high and wretched prospect.
Where is the one who planted vines that beanstalk out of their boxes?
Where is kindness its parishes its empty hand its open arms?
Over swells of lava over severe drops and quarter circles
swept out of the rock I'm compelled to witness the long days shorten.
Is it so that every world is only a world of enemies?
I've been here so long I think I hear my children passing the door.
Should I go to the door though there is only night and its garden
suddenly not my dream but hers and she dreams of us arriving.

#7 Larry's Castle

Elsewhere I slept as the rattle started like an engine that cranks
moans and whinnies but never starts or a wound clock whose key is lost.
No clock ticks in her room but if one speaks light fluently one can
tell the time by the shadow the fountain casts across the courtyard.
Hippocrates arrives again and I ask him what will happen.
Today is the day yes I guess and what am I to say to her
asleep he says but still aware a voice speaking a floor below
my voice warped into the scribble of a child in soot or lampblack
what kind of story do I tell apple is the longest story
I know let's see how does it go again apple apple apple.

PART TWO

Star World

Star World 1

I dug with the heels of my boots ingloriously gradual.
One afternoon we transplanted a rose bush that blossomed yearly
in memory of her mother to the middle of the garden
so she'd see it from the window if she raised her head to look out.
I dug against the bony earth the holly tree's nebulous roots
throughout the garden I slackened more than once her final winter
though we didn't know it yet the robins nesting in the branches
would be gone by summer when she returns to the room
      she looked from
lit up once by joy and light the room above which I cannot sleep.

Star World 2

A deep breath I am water tight on the ocean floor an egg cracks.
I proceed invincibly I dream alone and dauntless into
the realms of blue-headed wrasses sleeping the sleep of the fishes
dreaming with the rhizomatic samphire (*dreadful trade*)
     they once called
glasswort since with the opposite of water fire artisans
transform its ashes into glass on which Saint Peter smiles a smile
of light stopped on the window and speaks the opposite of water.

Star World 3

I walk into the night as it aches all over the countryside
tramping under the ruptured path of the milky way the moon-blue
swoop of the road pointed homeward say goodnight volcanic columns
so long rolling glens and valleys. The streetlights fur like hyacinths
like beacons and their intervals mentioning across the landscape
that war has come that villages are sacked that men lie in the mud
fortifications in ruins the howls of widows and orphans
like nettles the stinging of smoke and hours later when I awake
in my childhood bed there's embers dozing in the warm fireplace.

Star World 4

The troika platforms turbine through another boiling night of stars
of the distances between them of chaos which is nothingness
through the valley rolls a chaos. In the chaos of the night sky
I would find a key and keyhole a way out yes but into what
the strange passing from one blue world into another world of blue
most mysterious frequency since for so long no one could speak
of it and since when blue could be mentioned the old world was ended
by a new color of all things by indigo or common woad
by blue this most expensive shade the calm blue of hospice carpets
this blue by its presence welcomes the ritual of the new world.

Star World 5

The Colorado river ran and ran to shape the Grand Canyon
and now it is filled up with night right to the brim and more
night spills up to whatever is not night pulsars pulse I traverse
the chasm which is both nothing and rock around it sending back
one's voice the second guess of an echo which of the voices is my voice
how sarcasm offers two thoughts at once one inside the other.
My friends are scattered on ranges along the island's
        wave-wrecked coast
and turtle doves skidoo above mesas and yellow columbines.
She spends a final night at home. I have gone to rescue my friends.

Special World

Gnarly

I tried to make a monument out of the pink wisteria
and to shape from the lands of light cartilage from cartography
from rolling green and glowing plains and five-jointed
      springboard launchers
and vines that beanstalk from a box cumulus cumulonimbus
cirrus attended by sun dogs seen by ships at sea soon to sink
from forests of pupae furies of carnelian or ruby
from countless spiny crawling sprites duplicated as pathogens
from Osterberg and Orbison and Beethoven and Nine Inch Nails
from anthropomorphic stone heads in fortresses near far and wide
from falling dreams sweet streams that flow the length
      of the garden planted
with roses and honeysuckle with foxgloves and wild funguses
I tried to make a monument from the cathode rays blasting streams
of electrons behind a screen from quarries foxhunts and gunshots
from ghillies dipped low in Flecktarn scouting the forest on the hill
I want my monument to be composed of light you might say
so you can see it friend not things themselves but the seeing of them
the light stopping on them tree I adore you I adore you world.

Tubular

The roughed-off ends of pipes comprise a windless skyline citadel
as though they're waiting for music if someone had the breath for it
and anyway doesn't the wind distribute breath around the world
the wind never again striking her shoulders for those final breaths
I wasn't there we had driven to McDonald's of all places
the sun low on the carriageway *Diamonds on the Soles of Her Shoes*
on the radio and the rasp of the handbrake and the courtyard of gravel
the blue carpets of the hallways. With whatever strength she had left
she went without me as witness devotion I can't imagine.
I will myself to contain it: a paean laboring under
so many feet I have taken in a breath of the world so huge
the rest of my life will be spent breathing the world into the world.

Way Cool

I tried to make a monument from the television's On/Off
button whose once-black surface has been worn away to silver by
thousands of thumbs over the years and its hiss and buzz of static
a monument of its glass screen dense as bone or maybe the moon
or the shock of aspidistra in a pot of terracotta
on a mock Queen Anne side table or a needlework from Henry's
widow in Queensland in silver and gold depicting two dancers
dancing in the style of John Luke never never canst thou kiss.
The clock tick tocks at a gallop in the tiled cavern of the hall
sunset is drawn to the part-stained part-frosted glass of the front door.
Every other day I think I see her passing by the window
or crossing a bridge or walking ahead of me in the village
but this is the wrong universe among all the universes.

Awesome

A morning all of wintergreen the snow has closed the country roads
our house is white among the white fields the forest white on the hill
the river ripples freezing sines all the way to Solitude Bridge
to the main stream spume and spindrift the waters of the Irish Sea.
I walk for no reason along the middle of the purple road:
no traffic no people for miles and for no reason except for
being alone I try to scream into the wildness of the world.
I make no sound: the flakes of snow are noisier in their falling
the berries are loud with color on the back windowsill a bird
has written its name in footprints a handful of steps at the door.
The voice is made of whatever is left how the world is dented.
Dear friends I cannot rescue you any more than I can place her
shoulders in the way of the wind but when you're walking in the snow
when the time comes there's room for you in this voice
      because it's your voice.

Groovy

I tried to make a monument from the emptiness of the house:
the house in which everything starts the berries and scarps cactuses
inching along in the verdure mosses clinging to water pipes
but nothing would explain itself and things would only correspond.
The house empty but for me is a highway in the wilderness
is a river in the desert is a blue eye in the kettle
is a candle made of water is a photograph on fire
is a church bell in the graveyard is a letter I can't open
is a forest at Chernobyl is a beached whale at Donegal
is fair lined slippers for the cold is buckles of the purest gold
is the fox hunt stalking the fields is the fox guarding the henhouse
is the cat among the pigeons is the creak up in the rafters
when I returned to the empty house it was no longer empty.

Mondo

The waves the waves undulating the waves undulating flotsams
the waves undulating flotsams of belly-up fishes drowning
the poem is breathing underwater in the canals of Venice long
before I am born before she is married the gondolas cut
the glinting water the sun huge as she (young) orbits it the sound
of our river trickling up to the bridge and she hears it
sun-tempered waters of Venice fountains in the hospice courtyard
two Saturns of memory big jumble sale of the mind morphine
how much does this thing cost (darling) whatever do you call this thing?
In this her box of bric-à-brac a photo of a gondolier
a charm of blue Murano glass flashes of copper and cobalt
explaining themselves to the light. In the quietness of the house
the hush of the river running its capillary is sounded
in a voice like someone else's running away under the hills
where we can't follow communing with other waters emerging
as a torrent that spills into the lake it is my voice she hears.

Outrageous

So suddenly was the summer over like a bellows days shrank
the fireplace puffed out embers that flickered and soon extinguished
where over the hearth soot began to sign its name firewood sat
in a pile of splinters the tree tallest in the forest lightning
felled I went there to the forest on the hill behind our house
I frolicked and tramped through the mud to a place
   I thought no one else
had ever been before it was so deep into the wilderness
finding instead in a clearing hunters' leavings: cold fire pits
rusting tin cans the casings of distinct calibers of weapon
a fox hunt discarded passing through the fields like a noisy moon
the sparks of munitions lighting up their faces I imagine
some quarry in his den of earth the pillars of trees labyrinthine
witnesses: speak aloud these words the tall tree of the ear I put
my head against the fireplace that with a deep breath the embers
might confess to me what they've seen while the room fills up
   with their warmth.

Funky

The little sumo thunder gods shiko little bolts of lightning
the sky storm-dark as it has been these blue afternoons of winter
the garden is overgrowing a gooseberry splits on my tongue
full of the thinking of robins full of the odor of ozone.
I traveled back to other storms semibreves of rolling thunder
waiting finally for the flash a gooseberry splits on my tongue
and sixteen years have disappeared thousands of berries in the trees
like Christmases robins hop by their breasts a swell of ground rubies
while the roses swell and recede begonias swell and recede
homeless Saturn is halfway home the beautiful television
decomposes in a landfill the hard ground softens the soft ground
softens the hard ground the holly roots bristle suspended throughout
in the garden I buried my name I wanted it to be found.
Should I pray to gods of thunder or the wounded gods of myself
the storm crumbles the bank into the river and what can I say
this has not been easy thank you friend you are a super reader.

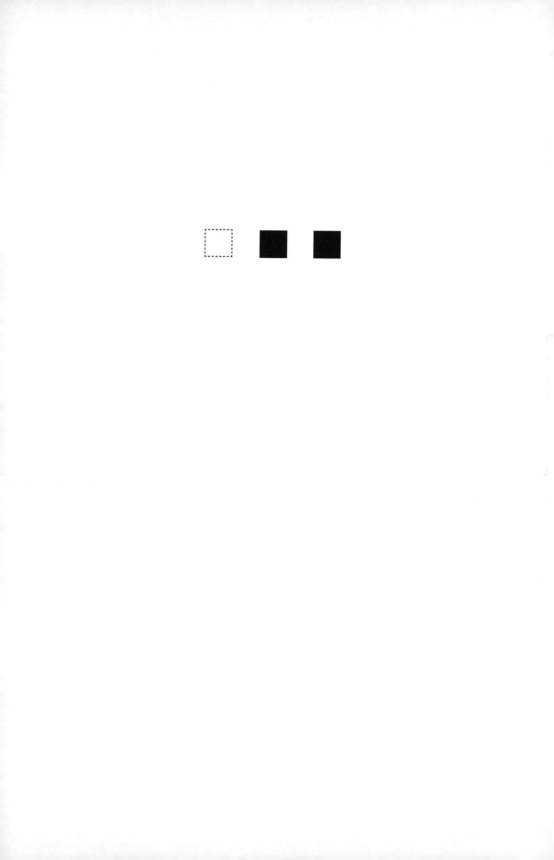

Front Door

In through the translucent panels of the front door stained with roses
here and there their green stems wander sun patterns the cavernous hall
with rose outlines the wood paneled box came sharp-cornered the TV
so heavy to look at it cut into my clavicle was it
full of cannonballs and was it carried on four or six or eight
sets of shoulders into the room such impossible heaviness
for the size of it and was it full of tinctures puzzled colors
picture elements their sweep rates flashing across it when I saw
my reflection in the blackness of its face it was a child's face.
Neighbors came over their fences a summer day but dark with storms:
a deluge impassible roads the forest lurching on the hill.
I felt my head turn into stone no it wasn't the old TV
we carried her to the window the meteors that time of year
Perseids only sparks really the Irish Sea fell from the sky
in bullets through the afternoon and Kong Kappa no King Koopa
navigates his ship through the storm an engine or thunder rumbles.
Electrons pooled under the clouds the room was heavy with ions.
I held my breath in the lightning the sea fell into the garden.
Evening rose like the river then the flash with all of us in it
and her voice moves around the edge of the world and now I think I
remember what I mean to say which is only to say that once
when all the world and love was young I saw it beautiful glowing
once in the corner of the room once I was sitting in its light.

THE END

CREDITS

(in order of appearance)

My house, Yoshi, hallucinogenic mushrooms (*Amanita muscaria*), mitosis, my mother, photography, light, the Lotus Position, economy, Kappa (Japanese mythological creature), television, Holly (*Ilex aquifolium*), Robins (*Erithacus rubecula*), Ivy (*Hedera*), Blackthorn (*Prunus spinosa*), Groundsel (*Senecio vulgaris*), Daisy (*Bellis perennis*), Petrarch (1304–1374), "Ascent of Mount Ventoux," my brother, Genoa, my father, turtle dove (*Streptopelia turtur*), things with spines, Saguaro cactus (*Carnegiea gigantean*), Bangor, swan pedalo, Chemotherapy, insomnia, Iggy and the Stooges, the Scoville Scale, Northern Ireland, Delftware, Lough Neagh, Sargasso Sea, eels, Sycamore (*Acer pseudo-platanus*), family photographs, Henry Smyth (d. 1964), Assisted Passage Migration Scheme, mining, mine collapse, Jacques Derrida, emeralds, Iron pyrite, stone cottages, Andrew Marvell (1621–1678), "The Garden," Michael Donaghy (1954–2004), "Haunts," Pigeon (*Columba palumbus*), Sparrow (*Passer domesticus*), William Shakespeare (1564–1616), *The Tempest*, Shepherds (singing), Wrasse (*Thalassoma bifasciatum*), Tilapia (*Oreochromis niloticus*), Hogfish (*Lachnolaimus maximus*), Dogfish (*Squalus acanthias*), Catfish (*Silurus glanis*), Salmon (*Salmo salar*), Tuna (*Thunnus thynnus*), Sunfish (*Mola mola*), Anglerfish (*Melanocetus johnsonii*), the Mariana Trench, Ulster Hospital, McDonald's, Nintendo Game Boy, Sagittarius, Carrick-a-Rede Rope Bridge, chestnuts, the First World War (1914–1918), acetone, cordite, Fairy Rings, a Surgeon, Surgery, Anesthesia, Johnny

Cash (1932–2003), "Dark as a Dungeon," Kimberly Diamond mine, South Africa, time, the Big Hole, rowboats, spelunking, Sharaska, alchemy, alternative therapies, climbing, Orpheus, childbirth, nurses' watch fobs, bats (*Pipistrellus pipistrellus*), Morphine, moonlight, Mercury, Salamander (*Salamandra salamandra*), Charon, Dante Alighieri (1265–1321), *The Divine Comedy*, vantage points, fox-hunting, Solitude Bridge, swans (*Cygnus olor*), trout (*Oncorhynchus mykiss*), bulrushes (*Typha latifolia*), gunfire, the Alps, edelweiss (*Leontopodium alpinum*), Ötzi the Iceman (d. c. 3500 BC), hop-hornbeam (*Ostrya carpinifolia*), flax (*Linum usitatissimum*), poppy (*Papaver somniferum*), Arion of Messina, dolphins, cithara, Coelacanth (*Latimeria chalumnae*), Lazarus of Bethany, Anemone (*Epiactis prolifera*), The Hospital, wizards, medical professionals, hemostatic medicines, opiates, video games, doppelgängers, Motörhead, Lemmy Kilminster (1945–2015), Pieter Bruegel (1525–1569), "Landscape with the Fall of Icarus," Virgil's *Eclogues*, Cracker Barrel (cheese), Ducks (*Anas platyrhynchos*), Cat (*Felis catus*), Donkey Kong, Cancer, Clouds, Baking, a biscuit tin, a river, the lake, Sunday, Fly-Fishing, Damselflies (*Ischnura heterosticta*), a walk to the lake, Scots Pine (*Pinus sylvestris L.*), Pylons, Herefords, Apple Blossom (*Malus domestica*), Goths, death, fashion, The Albert Bridge, rowers on the river Lagan, Starling (*Sturnus vulgaris*), Shigeru Miyamoto (1952–), Ludwig van Beethoven (1770–1827), "Fifth Symphony," Jasper, Carnelian, an ossuary, trills, piano, E-Flat Major, Virgin and Child, Forests, Charles Baudelaire (1821–1867), "Correspondances," Goat willow (*Salix caprea*), Caterpillar (*Agonopterix pallorella*), Camberwell Beauty (*Nymphalis antiopa*), Fishing, cruelty, underwater, the elements, synesthesia, Hedgehog (*Erinaceus europaeus*), metrical feet, Wood Mouse (*Apodemus sylvaticus*), Oboes, a clearing in the woods, first born children, mistreatment of animals, a white horse (*Equus ferus caballus*), convalescence, planting roses in the garden, amber, incense, gooseberries (*Ribes uva-crispa*), Ekphrasis, brook trout (*Salvelinus fontinalis*), a Spanish Galleon, explosives, The Omagh Bomb (15th August 1998), the Assumption of Mary, a funeral, half a century, St. Peter (d. 64), stained glass, color television, a Singer sewing machine, the radio, Roy Orbison (1936–1988), making curtains, Rhinoceros (*Rhinoceros unicornis*), basso ostinato, mountainous areas, the breakup of Pangaea, Dinosaurs, paleontology, Queensland, fossils, texts, Hale-Bopp, Storms in Spain, card games (Jack Change It), armor-plating, Albrecht Dürer (1471–1528), *Rhinoceros*, the imagination, recalcitrance, Eadweard Muybridge (1830–1904), *Sallie Gardner at a Gallop*, California, The Wright Brothers, Alphonse Pénaud (1850–1880), death, funeral, Super Nintendo Entertainment System, June, hospital, abdominal pain, Saturn Return, Hippocrates (c. 460– c. 370 B.C.), Albrecht Dürer (1471–1528), *Melencolia I*, angiogenesis inhibitors, Philip Larkin (1922–1985), "High Windows," precious stones, Francisco Goya (1746–1828), *Saturn Devouring His Son*, reverberation, cell destruction, bismuth, the Atacama Desert, eelgrass (*Zostera marina*), The La Mon Hotel, silence, kirtles, skeletons, sparks, sorry, palliative care, a hospice, Wendy O. Williams (1949–1998), Marie Celeste, New York, Ghost Ships, shipwreck, the Azores, mysteries, Philip Larkin (1922–1985), "The Whitsun Weddings," Memory, the Atlantic Ocean, becoming lost, secateurs, haircuts, mistaken identity, scissors, valleys, strata, mazes, dirt, visitors to the dying, a dripping fountain, choral music performed by birds, a telegram, letters, signature, funeral preparations, an old house, toy trains, ghosts, the shortness of life, first steps, first words, armor, stone-throwing, dismay, enmity, eternity, a future, a dream of us arriving, a failing engine, apples, Louis MacNeice (1907–1963), "Snow," rosebushes, robins, winter, in memoriam, grandmothers, digging, horticulture, fatigue, migration, wake, swimming, rebirth, sea creatures, sleeping with the fishes, artisans, William Shakespeare (1564–1616), *King Lear*, glasswort (*Crithmum maritimum*), stained glass, Pentecost, elemental forces, Vincent Van Gogh (1853–1890), *The Starry Night*, Anne Sexton (1928–1974), "The Starry Night," The Giant's Causeway, Co. Antrim, volcanoes, basalt, masquerades, Fancy Dress Parties, transmigration of the soul, the Milky Way, the moon, Zephyrus, hyacinths, sacked villages, a dream, the Colorado River, the Grand Canyon, thresholds of worlds, the color blue, indigo, woad, a Hospice, chaos pulsars, quasars, infinity, sarcasm, absent friends, mesas, columbines, nothing, monuments, memorials, wisteria (*Wisteria sinensis*), cartography, Jack and the Beanstalk, clouds, sun dogs (atmospheric phenomenon), sinking ships, pupae, carnelian, ruby, pathogens, James Newell Osterberg (b. 1947), Roy Orbison (1936–1988), Trent Reznor (b. 1965), falling dreams, Stranmillis, cathode rays, ghillie suits, Flecktarn, drainage pipes, plumbing, paeans, respiration, Paul Simon (1941–), "Diamonds on the Soles of Her Shoes," the death of my mother (1952–2012), televisions, thumbs, bone, moon, aspidistra, terracotta, Queen Anne (fashion), needlework, widows, John Luke (1906–1975), John Keats (1795–1821), clocks, sunset, the wrong universe, road closures, the Irish Sea, screaming, footprints in the snow, empty houses, The Uncanny, Chernobyl, beaching (of whales), Donegal, Christopher Marlowe (1564–1593), "The Passionate Shepherd to His Love," The Pastoral, tidal movements, Venice, breathing underwater, gondolas, Saturn (planet), gondoliers, Murano glass, William Shakespeare (1564–1616), *Othello*, lightning, felled trees, the forest behind my house, canned food, bullet casings, Rainer Maria Rilke (1875–1926), *Sonnets to Orpheus*, sumo wrestling, gooseberries (*Ribes uva-crispa*), time dilation, ozone, sixteen years, Christmas, begonias, landfills, thunder gods, most excellent and generous readers (you), the front door to my house, televisions, coffins, teamwork, weight, reflections, neighbors, heavy rain, the Perseids, King Koopa, Bowser, beautiful lights.

ACKNOWLEDGMENTS

So many thanks to Jefferson Holdridge, Alex Muller, and everyone at Wake Forest University Press for their enthusiasm, imagination, and kindness. Thank you to Peter Barnfather for his design. Thanks to Tracy Bohan and Katie Cacouris at The Wile Agency for their support and belief.

I'm grateful to Sally Rooney for publishing demo versions in *The Stinging Fly*, to Damian Smyth and the Arts Council of Northern Ireland, and to Maureen Kennelly, Paul Lenehan, and Elizabeth Mohen at Poetry Ireland for their encouragement and generosity, and to Emma Wright and Rachel Piercy and The Emma Press.

Thanks to colleagues and advisors at the Seamus Heaney Centre: Leontia Flynn, Gail McConnell, Fran Brearton, Glenn Patterson, Rachel Brown, Jimmy McAleavey, and Nick Laird, and to Colin Graham, Edna and Michael Longley, Paula Meehan, Theo Dorgan, and Paul Maddern. Particular thanks to Sinéad Morrissey for her brilliance, and for helping me understand what I was trying to say, and to *il professore, il maestro*, Ciaran Carson, to whom I am indebted and to whom language itself is indebted.

Much gratitude to Padraig Regan for their imagination and for many conversations, to Daire Moffat, Michael Magee, Tom Morris, Stephen Connolly, Manuela Moser, Tara McEvoy, Caitlin Newby, Dane Holt, Sacha White, Scott McKendry, Andy Eaton, Dave Coates, Darragh

McCausland, Cal Doyle, Wayne Miller, and to Mary Denvir and the legend of Bookfinders Café, and of course to these boys: Nathan Lynch, James Gilpin, Michael Weir, John Culbert, Ryan Wiles.

Love to Bríd, always.